Pebble® Plus

ALL ABOUT WINTER

Snowflakes

by Martha E. H. Rustad

Consulting Editor: Gail Saunders-Smith, PhD

Capstone press®

Mankato, Minnesota

Pebble Plus is published by Capstone Press,
151 Good Counsel Drive, P.O. Box 669, Mankato, Minnesota 56002.
www.capstonepress.com

1 2 3 4 5 6 13 12 11 10 09 08

Library of Congress Cataloging-in-Publication Data
Rustad, Martha E. H. (Martha Elizabeth Hillman), 1975–
    Snowflakes / by Martha E. H. Rustad.
    p. cm. — (Pebble plus. All about winter)
    Summary: "Simple text and photographs present snowflakes" — Provided by publisher.
    Includes bibliographical references and index.
    ISBN-13: 978-1-4296-2202-8 (hardcover)
    ISBN-10: 1-4296-2202-4 (hardcover)
    1. Snowflakes — Juvenile literature. I. Title. II. Series.
QC926.37R875 2009
551.57'841 — dc22

2008003337

Editorial Credits
Sarah L. Schuette, editor; Veronica Bianchini, designer; Marcie Spence, photo researcher

Photo Credits
BigStockPhoto.com, 7
Capstone Press/Karon Dubke, cover, 11
Getty Images Inc./Ariel Skelley, 17; Roine Magnusson/Stone, 9
Shutterstock/Arlene Jean Gee, 13; Christina Richards, 21; Elena Elisseeva, 5; Martine Oger, 15;
    Mehmet Dilsia, 19; Timothy Epp, 1

Note to Parents and Teachers

The All about Winter set supports national science standards related to changes during
the seasons. This book describes and illustrates snowflakes. The images support
early readers in understanding the text. The repetition of words and phrases helps early
readers learn new words. This book also introduces early readers to subject-specific
vocabulary words, which are defined in the Glossary section. Early readers may need
assistance to read some words and to use the Table of Contents, Glossary, Read More,
Internet Sites, and Index sections of the book.

Table of Contents

What Are Snowflakes?

Snowflakes are small pieces
of frozen water.

Each snowflake is different.

All snowflakes have six sides.
Snowflakes can be
big or small.

When It Snows

Snowflakes fall
from clouds.
They cover everything
in a blanket of snow.

Dry and fluffy snowflakes
fall in very cold temperatures.
Wet and heavy snowflakes
fall in warmer temperatures.

Lightly falling snowflakes
are called snow showers.
Big storms with lots
of snow and wind
are blizzards.

In the Snow

We work in the snow.

Jim shovels the snow

from his sidewalk.

We play in the snow.

Sam builds a snowman.

Joe and his mom
ride a sled down
a snowy hill.

Melting

Snowflakes melt when
the weather gets warmer.
Spring is coming!

Glossary

blizzard — a heavy snowstorm with strong wind; a blizzard can last several days.

spring — the season between winter and summer; the weather becomes warmer and the days get longer.

temperature — the measure of how hot or cold something is

weather — the condition outdoors at a certain time and place; weather changes with each season.